african

HEARTWARMING FLAVOURS FROM A TRADITIONAL CUISINE

rosamund grant

southwater

This edition is published by Southwater

Southwater is an imprint of Anness Publishing Ltd
Hermes House, 88–89 Blackfriars Road, London SE1 8HA
tel. 020 7401 2077; fax 020 7633 9499
www.southwaterbooks.com; info@anness.com

This edition distributed in the UK by The Manning Partnership Ltd, 6 The Old Dairy, Melcombe Road, Bath BA2 3LR; tel. 01225 478 444; fax 01225 478 440; sales@manning-partnership.co.uk

This edition distributed in the USA and Canada by National Book Network, 4720 Boston Way, Lanham, MD 20706; tel. 301 459 3366; fax 301 459 1705; www.nbnbooks.com

This edition distributed in Australia by Pan Macmillan Australia, Level 18, St Martins Tower, 31 Market St, Sydney, NSW 2000; tel. 1300 135 113; fax 1300 135 103; customer.service@macmillan.com.au

This edition distributed in New Zealand by The Five Mile Press (NZ) Ltd, PO Box 33–1071 Takapuna, Unit 11/101–111 Diana Drive, Glenfield, Auckland 10; tel. (09) 444 4144; fax (09) 444 4518; fivemilenz@clear.net.nz

Publisher Joanna Lorenz
Managing Editor Linda Fraser
Project Editor Zoe Antoniou
Designer Ian Sandom
Illustrations Madeleine David
Photography and styling Patrick McLeavey
Food for photography Annie Nichols
Jacket photography Thomas Odulate
Production Controller Joanna King

Printed and bound in Singapore

For all recipes, quantities are given in both metric and imperial measures, and, where appropriate, measures are also given in standard cups and spoons. Follow one set, but not a mixture, because they are not interchangeable.

Pictures on frontispiece: Lamb Tagine (top), and Spiced Fried Lamb with Ethiopian Collard Greens (bottom).

5 7 9 10 8 6 4

african

Contents

INTRODUCTION

Entertaining with food and music is integral to African social life, and family, friends and festivity are closely associated in both rural and urban homes. "No advance warning required" is an attitude that prevails and, in fact, cooking only for the members of your household can get you a bad reputation! So, many hosts and hostesses make it their business to ensure that there are always extra titbits around for unexpected visitors who might call by at any time.

Rigid recipes are rare; most African cooks inherit vague techniques by word of mouth and then go on to develop their skills by experimenting with different ingredients and cooking methods. They often create new and interesting combinations by following their instincts rather than written instructions. So it isn't too fanciful to talk about cooking that comes from the heart.

In some African countries, soup is the whole meal, made using meat or fish and dried beans or vegetables, and served with a staple food such as *fu fu* (ground rice) or boiled yam. Main courses are dominated by tasty and interesting fish and shellfish, which is found in abundance around the coast or by lakes. There are more than 200 types of fish in Nigeria alone. In some regions, meat and fish are scarce and only eaten on festive occasions, but economic restraints do not prevent Africa's many gourmets from creating delectable dishes. Meat is usually cooked in spicy sauces, and is frequently flavoured with smoked fish or dried prawns.

Throughout Africa, vegetable, bean and lentil dishes are very popular and meat is often used as one of a number of flavourings, rather than as a main ingredient. For dessert or snacks throughout the day, there is a wonderful array of tropical fruits, such as mangoes and pawpaw, which are a familiar sight.

Eating in Africa is a unique and exciting experience, shaped by local traditions and customs which makes cooking fun and experimental. For above all, cooking the African way is about having a feel for the food.

Opposite: Tropical Fruit Pancakes, and Pawpaw and Mango with Mango Cream.

INGREDIENTS

There are many ingredients that are used in African cooking that may be unfamiliar. Most, however, can be found in large supermarkets, street markets and in African and Asian stores, which often stock a huge variety of fresh fruit and vegetables.

One of the most common flavours to be found is that of the chilli, which is often used to add spice to a recipe. The potency of this ingredient varies dramatically, with one of the hottest

Above (clockwise from top left): yams, okra, christophene, sweet potatoes. Above right: mung beans, black-eyed beans, cardamom pods (just showing), egusi, ground egusi.

chillies being the Scotch Bonnet. Even adventurous cooks should accustom themselves slowly to the zingingly hot dishes in which Africans specialize and revel! If you do not want fiery food, remove the seeds and core of chillies and add little by little.

Less well-known are the oils, such as palm oil, which is unlike any other oil and should be used sparingly – its distinctive, strong flavour is an acquired taste. Groundnut oil is made from peanuts and this is also essential if you want to achieve an authentic African taste, while groundnut paste is used to make sauces or the delicious Groundnut Soup. If the paste is difficult to find, replace it with natural smooth or crunchy peanut butter. Careful experimentation is the key to enjoying these ingredients.

African cooks prepare lots of recipes using vegetables and pulses, and for many people these are the mainstay of their diet.

Yams and sweet potatoes are some of the staple vegetables that make superb dishes. They come in many shapes and sizes and the flesh is either yellow or white. Plantains, members of the banana family, are also essential. All of these are delicious boiled, roasted, baked, mashed or made into chips, and are enjoyed in both sweet and savoury dishes.

There are also many other commonly enjoyed vegetables. Christophene is pear-shaped with a cream-coloured or green skin. It has a bland flavour, similar to squash or marrow. Alternatively, cassava is a tropical vegetable with tuberous roots and a brown skin with hard starchy white flesh. Dried and ground it makes cassava flour and gari, a flour used in various recipes. Egusi, which is also ground and added to many dishes, is made from either melon seed or the seeds of a fruit that is a cross between a gourd and a pumpkin. Aubergines and okra are also popular. Choose small firm okra when you are shopping, and wash and dry them before topping, tailing and cutting, as this will prevent them from getting too sticky.

Pulses are common in most recipes. Black-eyed beans, for example, originally came from Africa where it is a staple food. They can be soaked overnight or boiled without soaking, if an extra half hour is added to the cooking time. They are used in all sorts of soups, stews, rice dishes, salads and snacks. Also there are mung beans, sometimes known as green or golden gram, which are small, bright green dried beans. Red kidney beans are

Above: a selection of green bananas and plantains.

also common. Care should be taken when preparing these in particular: they can be poisonous when raw and should be soaked for several hours or overnight, and then boiled rapidly for 10-15 minutes before simmering until tender, or cooked according to the recipe.

Market stalls are full of luscious fruit – pineapples, coconuts, mangoes and spicy-smelling guavas – and it is not unusual for fruit trees to grow in people's gardens, there just for the picking. Herbs such as coriander and spices such as allspice add an extra dimension, so that traditional African cuisine makes for an interesting and delicious culinary adventure.

VEGETABLE SOUP WITH COCONUT

he mild, creamy flavour of coconut makes this a vegetable soup for everyone to enjoy all year round.

INGREDIENTS

175g/6oz each turnip, sweet potato and pumpkin
25g/1oz/2 tbsp butter or margarine
1/2 red onion, finely chopped
5ml/1 tsp dried marjoram
2.5ml/1/2 tsp ground ginger
1.5ml/1/4 tsp ground cinnamon
15ml/1 tbsp chopped spring onion
1 litre/1 3/4 pints/4 cups well-flavoured vegetable stock
30ml/2 tbsp flaked almonds
1 fresh chilli, seeded and chopped
5ml/1 tsp sugar
25g/1oz creamed coconut
salt and freshly ground black pepper
chopped coriander (optional)

SERVES 4

1 Peel the turnip, sweet potato and pumpkin. Chop into medium-size dice.

2 Melt the butter or margarine in a large non-stick saucepan. Fry the onion for 4–5 minutes. Add the diced vegetables and fry for 3–4 minutes.

3 Add the marjoram, ginger, cinnamon, spring onion, salt and pepper to the pan. Fry over a low heat for about 10 minutes, stirring frequently.

4 Add the vegetable stock, flaked almonds, chopped chilli and sugar and stir well to mix, then cover and simmer gently for about 10–15 minutes, or until all the vegetables are just tender.

5 Grate the creamed coconut into the soup and stir to mix. Sprinkle with chopped coriander, if liked, then spoon into warmed bowls and serve.

PLANTAIN AND CORN SOUP

P lantains in African cooking are a very popular ingredient, and here they combine with sweetcorn to make a hearty soup.

INGREDIENTS

25g/1oz/2 tbsp butter or margarine
1 onion, finely chopped
1 garlic clove, crushed
275g/10oz yellow plantains, peeled and sliced
1 large tomato, peeled and chopped
175g/6oz/1 cup sweetcorn
5ml/1 tsp dried tarragon, crushed
900ml/1½ pints/3¾ cups vegetable or chicken stock
1 green chilli, seeded and chopped
pinch of grated nutmeg
salt and freshly ground black pepper

SERVES 4

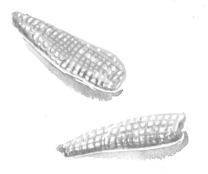

1 Melt the butter or margarine in a saucepan over a moderate heat, add the onion and garlic and fry for a few minutes until the onion is soft.

2 Add the plantain, tomato and sweetcorn and cook for 5 minutes.

3 Add the dried tarragon, vegetable or chicken stock, chilli and salt and pepper, and simmer for 10 minutes, or until the plantain is tender. Stir in the nutmeg and serve at once.

GROUNDNUT SOUP

Groundnuts (or peanuts), are very widely used in sauces in African cooking. You'll find groundnut paste in health food shops – it makes a wonderfully rich soup, but you could use peanut butter instead if you prefer. Traditionally the okra are chopped, which gives the soup a slightly "tacky" consistency.

INGREDIENTS

45ml/3 tbsp pure groundnut paste
or peanut butter
1.5 litres/2¹/₂ pints/6¹/₄ cups stock
or water
30ml/2 tbsp tomato purée
1 onion, chopped
2 slices fresh root ginger
1.5ml/¹/₄ tsp dried thyme
1 bay leaf
salt and chilli powder
225g/8oz white yam, diced
10 small okra, trimmed (optional)

SERVES 4

1 Place the groundnut paste or peanut butter in a mixing bowl and pour in 300ml/¹/₂ pint/1¹/₄ cups of the stock or water and the tomato purée. Blend together to make a smooth paste.

2 Spoon the nut mixture into a saucepan and add the onion, ginger, thyme, bay leaf, salt, chilli and the remaining stock.

3 Heat gently until simmering, then cook for 1 hour, stirring from time to time to prevent the nut mixture sticking.

4 Add the white yam cubes, cook for a further 10 minutes, then add the okra, if using, and simmer until both are tender. Serve at once.

LAMB, BEAN AND PUMPKIN SOUP

Black-eyed beans can be bought in health food stores and most supermarkets. Soak them overnight before preparing this tasty soup.

INGREDIENTS
115g/4oz split black-eyed beans, soaked overnight
675g/1¹/₂lb neck of lamb, cut into medium-size chunks
5ml/1 tsp chopped fresh thyme, or 2.5ml/¹/₂ tsp dried
2 bay leaves
1.2 litres/2 pints/5 cups stock or water
1 onion, sliced
225g/8oz pumpkin, diced
2 black cardamom pods
7.5ml/1¹/₂ tsp ground turmeric
15ml/1 tbsp chopped fresh coriander
2.5ml/¹/₂ tsp caraway seeds
1 fresh green chilli, seeded and chopped
2 green bananas
1 carrot
salt and freshly ground black pepper

SERVES 4

1 Drain the black-eyed beans thoroughly, place them in a saucepan and cover them with fresh cold water.

2 Bring the beans to the boil, boil rapidly for 10 minutes and then reduce the heat and simmer, covered, for 40–50 minutes until tender, adding more water if necessary. Remove from the heat and set aside to cool.

3 Meanwhile, put the lamb in a large saucepan, add the thyme, bay leaves and stock or water and bring to the boil. Cover and simmer over a moderate heat for 1 hour, or until tender.

4 Add the onion, pumpkin, cardamom pods, turmeric, coriander, caraway, chilli and seasoning and stir. Bring back to a simmer and then cook, uncovered, for 15 minutes, until the pumpkin is tender, stirring occasionally.

5 When the beans are cool, spoon them into a blender or food processor with their liquid and blend to a smooth purée.

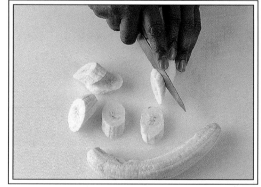

6 Cut the bananas into medium slices and the carrot into thin slices. Stir into the soup with the black-eyed beans and cook for 10–12 minutes, until the vegetables are tender. Adjust the seasoning and serve.

YAM BALLS

Yam balls are a popular snack in many African countries. They are traditionally made quite plain, but can be flavoured with chopped vegetables and herbs as in this recipe, or with cooked meat or fish, or spices.

INGREDIENTS

450g/1lb white yam
30ml/2 tbsp finely chopped onion
45ml/3 tbsp chopped tomatoes
2.5ml/¹/₂ tsp chopped fresh thyme
1 green chilli, finely chopped
15ml/1 tbsp finely chopped spring onion
1 garlic clove, crushed
1 egg, beaten
oil, for shallow frying
seasoned flour, for dusting
salt and freshly ground black pepper
lettuce, to serve

MAKES ABOUT 24 BALLS

1 Peel the yam, cut it into pieces and boil in salted water for about 30 minutes, or until tender. Drain and mash.

2 Add the onion, tomatoes, thyme, chilli, spring onion and garlic, then stir in the egg and seasoning and mix well.

3 Using a dessertspoon, scoop the mixture out and mould into balls. Heat some oil in a frying pan, roll the balls in the seasoned flour and then fry for a few minutes, in batches, until golden brown. Drain on kitchen paper. Serve hot on a bed of lettuce.

COOK'S TIP
If you like, add fresh chopped herbs to the yam mixture; parsley and chives make a good combination. Mix in 30ml/2 tbsp with the egg and seasoning.

TATALE

ver-ripe plantains are never thrown away and in Ghana they are often used to make this well-loved snack.

INGREDIENTS
2 over-ripe plantains
25–50g/1–2oz/2–4 tbsp self-raising flour
1 small onion, finely chopped
1 egg, beaten
5ml/1 tsp palm oil (optional)
salt
1 fresh green chilli, seeded and chopped
oil, for shallow frying
watercress, to garnish

SERVES 4

1 Peel and mash the plantains. Place them in a bowl and add enough flour to bind, stirring thoroughly.

2 Add the onion, egg, palm oil, if using, salt and chilli. Mix well and leave to stand for 20 minutes.

3 Heat some oil in a frying pan. Spoon in dessertspoons of mixture and fry in batches for 3–4 minutes until golden, turning once. Drain on kitchen paper. Serve hot or cold garnished with watercress.

SPICY KEBABS

hese spicy kebabs taste wonderful on their own, or you could serve them with a spicy dip.

INGREDIENTS

450g/1lb minced beef
1 egg
3 garlic cloves, crushed
½ onion, finely chopped
2.5ml/½ tsp freshly ground black pepper
7.5ml/1½ tsp ground cumin
7.5ml/1½ tsp dhania (ground coriander)
5ml/1 tsp ground ginger
10ml/2 tsp garam masala
15ml/1 tbsp lemon juice
50–75g/2–3oz/1–1½ cups fresh
white breadcrumbs
1 small chilli, seeded and chopped
oil, for deep frying
salt and freshly ground black pepper
lettuce leaves, to serve

MAKES 18–20 BALLS

1 Place the minced beef in a large bowl and add the egg, garlic, onion, spices, seasoning, lemon juice, about 50g/2oz/1 cup of the breadcrumbs and the chilli.

2 Using your hands or a wooden spoon, mix the ingredients together until the mixture is firm. If it feels sticky, add more of the breadcrumbs and mix again until firm.

3 Heat the oil in a large heavy-based pan or deep-fat fryer. Shape the mixture into balls or fingers and fry, a few at a time, for 5 minutes or until well browned all over.

4 Using a slotted spoon, drain the kebabs and then transfer to a plate lined with kitchen paper. Cook the remaining kebabs in the same way and then serve them all on a bed of lettuce leaves.

EAST AFRICAN ROAST CHICKEN

A spicy marinade turns a chicken into something very special – serve with rice and a fresh salad for a complete meal.

INGREDIENTS

1.75kg/4–4½ lb chicken
30ml/2 tbsp softened butter, plus extra
for basting
3 garlic cloves, crushed
5ml/1 tsp freshly ground black pepper
5ml/1 tsp ground turmeric
2.5ml/½ tsp ground cumin
5ml/1 tsp dried thyme
15ml/1 tbsp finely chopped
fresh coriander
60ml/4 tbsp thick coconut milk
60ml/4 tbsp medium-dry sherry
5ml/1 tsp tomato purée
salt and chilli powder
sprigs of fresh coriander, to garnish

SERVES 6

1 Remove the giblets from the chicken, if necessary, rinse out the cavity and pat the skin dry.

2 Put the butter and all the remaining ingredients in a bowl and mix together to form a thick paste.

3 Gently ease the skin of the chicken away from the flesh and rub generously with the herb and butter mixture. Rub more of the mixture over the skin, legs and wings of the chicken and into the neck cavity.

4 Place the chicken in a roasting tin, cover loosely with foil and marinate overnight in the fridge.

5 Preheat the oven to 190°C/375°F/Gas 5. Cover the chicken with clean foil and roast for 1 hour, then turn the chicken over and baste with the pan juices. Cover again with foil and cook for 30 minutes.

6 Remove the foil and place the chicken breast-side up. Rub it with extra butter and roast for a further 10–15 minutes, until the meat juices run clear and the skin is golden brown. Serve, garnished with plenty of fresh coriander.

YASSA CHICKEN

Senegalese cooks make wonderful *Yassa*. Instead of frying, they often grill the chicken before adding it to the sauce. For a less tangy flavour, you can add less lemon juice, although it does mellow after cooking.

INGREDIENTS

150ml/¼ pint/⅔ cup lemon juice
60ml/4 tbsp malt vinegar
3 onions, sliced
60ml/4 tbsp groundnut or vegetable oil
1kg/2¼lb chicken pieces
2 thyme sprigs
1 green chilli, seeded and finely chopped
2 bay leaves
425ml/¾ pint/1⅞ cups chicken stock

SERVES 4

1 Mix the lemon juice, vinegar, onions and 30ml/2 tbsp of the oil together. Place the chicken pieces in a shallow dish and pour over the lemon mixture. Cover with clear film and leave to marinate for 3 hours.

2 Heat the remaining oil in a large saucepan and fry the chicken pieces for 4–5 minutes until browned.

3 Add the marinated onions to the chicken. Fry for 3 minutes, then add the marinade, thyme, chilli, bay leaves and half of the stock.

4 Cover the pan and simmer gently over a moderate heat for about 35 minutes, until the chicken is cooked through, adding more stock as the sauce evaporates. Serve hot.

JOLOFF CHICKEN AND RICE

erve this well-known, colourful West African dish at a dinner party or other special occasion.

INGREDIENTS

1kg/2¼lb chicken, cut into 4–6 pieces
2 garlic cloves, crushed
5ml/1 tsp dried thyme
30ml/2 tbsp palm or vegetable oil
400g/14oz can chopped tomatoes
15ml/1 tbsp tomato purée
1 onion, chopped
450ml/¾ pint/1⅞ cups chicken stock or water
30ml/2 tbsp dried shrimps or crayfish, ground
1 green chilli, seeded and finely chopped
350g/12oz/1½ cups long grain rice, washed
fresh or dried thyme, to garnish

SERVES 4

1 Rub the chicken with the garlic and thyme and set aside.

2 Heat the oil in a saucepan until hazy, then add the chopped tomatoes, tomato purée and onion. Cook over a moderately high heat for about 15 minutes, until the tomatoes are well reduced, stirring occasionally at first and then more frequently as the tomatoes thicken.

3 Reduce the heat a little, add the chicken pieces and stir well to coat with the sauce. Cook for 10 minutes, stirring, then add the stock or water, the dried shrimps or crayfish and the chilli. Bring to the boil and simmer for 5 minutes, stirring occasionally.

4 Put the rice in a separate saucepan. Scoop 300ml/½ pint/1¼ cups of the sauce into a measuring jug, top up with water to 450ml/¾ pint/1⅞ cups and stir into the rice.

5 Cook the rice, covered, until the liquid is absorbed, then place a piece of foil on top of the rice, cover the pan with a lid and cook over a low heat for 20 minutes, or until the rice is cooked, adding water if needed.

6 Transfer the chicken pieces to a warmed serving plate. Simmer the sauce until reduced by half. Pour over the chicken and serve with the rice, garnished with thyme.

CHICKEN WITH MUNG BEANS

K*uku*, this delicious tangy chicken stew, comes from Kenya. The amount of lemon juice can be reduced if you prefer a less sharp sauce.

INGREDIENTS

6 chicken thighs or pieces
2.5–4ml/½ – ⅔ tsp ground ginger
50g/2oz mung beans
60ml/4 tbsp corn oil
2 onions, finely chopped
2 garlic cloves, crushed
5 tomatoes, peeled and chopped
1 green chilli, seeded and finely chopped
30ml/2 tbsp lemon juice
300ml/½ pint/1¼ cups coconut milk
300ml/½ pint/1¼ cups water
15ml/1 tbsp chopped fresh coriander
salt and freshly ground black pepper
green vegetables, cooked rice and chapatis, to serve

SERVES 4–6

1 Season the chicken pieces with the ground ginger and a little salt and pepper, then set aside in a cool place to marinate. Meanwhile, boil the mung beans in plenty of water for 35 minutes until soft, then mash well.

2 Heat the oil in a large saucepan over a moderate heat and fry the chicken pieces, in batches if necessary, until they are evenly browned. Transfer them to a plate and set aside, reserving the oil and chicken juices in the pan.

3 In the same pan, fry the onions and garlic for 5 minutes, then add the tomatoes and chilli and cook for a further 1–2 minutes, stirring well.

4 Add the mashed mung beans, lemon juice and coconut milk to the pan. Simmer for 5 minutes, then add the chicken pieces and a little water if the sauce is too thick. Stir in the coriander and simmer for about 35 minutes, or until the chicken is cooked through. Serve with green vegetables, rice and chapatis.

KOFTA CURRY

lthough fiddly, koftas are worth making. You can prepare them in advance and chill until needed.

INGREDIENTS
450g/1lb minced beef or lamb
45ml/3 tbsp finely chopped onion
15ml/1 tbsp chopped fresh coriander
15ml/1 tbsp natural yogurt
about 60ml/4 tbsp plain flour
10ml/2 tsp ground cumin
5ml/1 tsp garam masala
5ml/1 tsp ground turmeric
5ml/1 tsp dhania (ground coriander)
1 green chilli, seeded and finely chopped
2 garlic cloves, crushed
1.5ml/¼ tsp black mustard seeds
1 egg (optional)
salt and freshly ground black pepper

FOR THE CURRY SAUCE
30ml/2 tbsp ghee or butter
1 onion, finely chopped
2 garlic cloves, crushed
45ml/3 tbsp curry powder
4 green cardamom pods
600ml/1 pint/2½ cups chicken stock
15ml/1 tbsp tomato purée
30ml/2 tbsp natural yogurt
15ml/1 tbsp chopped fresh coriander
cooked rice and coriander, to serve

SERVES 4

1 Put the minced beef or lamb into a large bowl, add all the remaining meatball ingredients and mix well with your hands. Roll the mixture into small balls and put aside on a floured plate until required.

2 To make the curry sauce, heat the ghee or butter in a saucepan over a moderate heat and fry the chopped onion and garlic for about 10 minutes, or until the onion is soft and buttery.

3 Reduce the heat, then add the curry powder and cardamom pods and cook for a few minutes, stirring well.

4 Slowly stir in the stock, then add the tomato purée, yogurt and coriander and stir well. Simmer for 10 minutes.

5 Add the koftas a few at a time, cook briefly and then add a few more, until all are in the pan. Simmer, uncovered, for about 20 minutes, or until the koftas are cooked. Avoid stirring, but gently shake the pan occasionally to move the koftas around.

6 The curry should thicken slightly, but if it is too dry add more stock or water. Serve hot on rice, garnished with coriander.

LAMB TAGINE WITH CORIANDER AND SPICES

Here is Rachida Mounti's version of a Moroccan-style tagine. It can be made with chops or cutlets, and either marinated or cooked immediately after seasoning.

INGREDIENTS
4 lamb chump chops
2 garlic cloves, crushed
pinch of saffron strands
2.5ml/½ tsp ground cinnamon, plus extra to garnish
2.5ml/½ tsp ground ginger
15ml/1 tbsp chopped fresh coriander
15ml/1 tbsp chopped fresh parsley
1 onion, finely chopped
45ml/3 tbsp olive oil
300ml/½ pint/1¼ cups lamb stock
50g/2oz/½ cup blanched almonds
5ml/1 tsp sugar
salt and freshly ground black pepper
cooked rice and bread, to serve

SERVES 4

1 Season the lamb with the garlic, saffron, cinnamon, ginger and a little salt and black pepper. Place on a large plate and sprinkle with the coriander, parsley and onion. Cover loosely and set aside in the fridge for a few hours to marinate.

2 Heat the oil in a large frying pan over a moderate heat. Add the marinated lamb and all the herbs and onion from the dish.

3 Fry for 1–2 minutes, turning once, then add the stock, bring to the boil and simmer gently for 30 minutes, turning the chops once.

4 Meanwhile, heat a small frying pan over a moderate heat, add the almonds and dry fry until golden, shaking the pan occasionally to ensure they colour evenly. Transfer to a bowl and set aside.

5 Transfer the chops to a serving plate and keep warm. Increase the heat under the pan and boil the sauce until reduced by about half. Stir in the sugar. Pour the sauce over the chops, arrange on a bed of rice and sprinkle with the fried almonds and a little extra ground cinnamon. Serve immediately with fresh bread to mop up the juices.

COOK'S TIP
Lamb Tagine is a fragrant dish originating in North Africa. It is traditionally made in a cooking dish, known as a tagine, from where it takes its name. This dish consists of a plate with a tall lid with sloping sides. It has a narrow opening to let steam escape, while retaining the flavour.

NIGERIAN MEAT STEW

This recipe was adapted from a Nigerian stew. It is made with meats of different flavours, such as beef, offal and mutton, along with dried fish or snails, and served with yam or rice.

INGREDIENTS

675g/1½lb oxtail, chopped
450g/1lb stewing beef, cubed
450g/1lb skinless, boneless chicken
breasts, chopped
2 garlic cloves, crushed
1½ onions
30ml/2 tbsp palm or vegetable oil
30ml/2 tbsp tomato purée
400g/14oz can plum tomatoes
2 bay leaves
5ml/1 tsp dried thyme
5ml/1 tsp mixed spice
salt and freshly ground black pepper

SERVES 4–6

1 Place the oxtail in a large saucepan, cover with water and bring to the boil. Skim the surface of any froth, then cover and cook for 1½ hours, adding more water as necessary.

2 Add the beef and continue to cook for a further hour, until tender.

3 Meanwhile, season the chicken breasts with the crushed garlic and roughly chop one onion.

4 Heat the oil in a large saucepan over a moderate heat and fry the chopped onion for about 5 minutes until soft. Stir in the tomato purée, cook briskly for a few minutes, then add the chicken. Stir well and cook gently for 5 minutes.

5 Meanwhile, place the plum tomatoes and the remaining half onion in a food processor or blender and blend to a purée. Stir into the chicken mixture with the bay leaves, thyme, mixed spice and seasoning.

6 Add about 600ml/1 pint/2½ cups of stock from the cooked oxtail and beef and simmer for 35 minutes.

7 Add the oxtail and beef to the chicken. Heat gently, adjust the seasoning and serve hot.

SPICED FRIED LAMB

An Ethiopian dish, *Awaze Tibs*, is flavoured with a red pepper spice mixture called berbiri, which is traditionally made from a variety of East African herbs and spices. This version uses spices that are a little easier to find!

INGREDIENTS
450g/1lb lamb fillet
45ml/3 tbsp olive oil
1 red onion, sliced
2.5ml/½ tsp grated fresh root ginger
2 garlic cloves, crushed
½ green chilli, seeded and finely chopped (optional)
15ml/1 tbsp clarified butter or ghee
salt and freshly ground black pepper
cabbage and red pepper strips, to serve

FOR THE BERBIRI
2.5ml/½ tsp each chilli powder, paprika, ground ginger, ground cinnamon, ground cardamom seeds and dried basil
5ml/1 tsp garlic granules

SERVES 4

1 To make the berbiri, combine all the ingredients in a small bowl and tip into an airtight container. Berbiri will keep for several months if stored in a cool dry place.

2 Trim the meat of any fat, then cut into 2cm/¾in cubes.

3 Heat the oil in a large frying pan and fry the meat and onion for 5–6 minutes, until the meat is browned on all sides.

4 Add the ginger and garlic to the pan and 10ml/2 tsp of the berbiri, then stir-fry over a brisk heat for a further 5–10 minutes.

5 Add the chilli, if using, and season well. Stir in the butter or ghee just before serving with cabbage and red peppers.

MUTTON WITH BLACK-EYED BEANS AND PUMPKIN

Cooking meat together with vegetables, especially beans, is very common in African cooking. The pumpkin brings a lovely sweetness to this dish. Serve it with boiled yam, plantains or sweet potatoes.

INGREDIENTS

450g/1lb boneless lean mutton or
lamb, cubed
1 litre/1¾ pints/4 cups chicken or lamb
stock or water
75g/3oz/½ cup black-eyed beans,
soaked overnight
1 onion, chopped
2 garlic cloves, crushed
40ml/2½ tbsp tomato purée
7.5ml/1½ tsp dried thyme
7.5ml/1½ tsp palm or vegetable oil
5ml/1 tsp mixed spice
2.5ml/½ tsp freshly ground black pepper
115g/4oz pumpkin, chopped
salt and a little hot pepper sauce

SERVES 4

1 Put the mutton or lamb in a large pan with the stock or water and bring to the boil. Skim off any foam, then reduce the heat, cover and simmer for 1 hour.

2 Stir in the drained black-eyed beans and continue cooking for about 35 minutes.

3 Add the onion, garlic, tomato purée, dried thyme, oil, mixed spice, ground black pepper, salt and hot pepper sauce, and cook for a further 15 minutes, or until the beans are tender.

4 Add the pumpkin and simmer gently for 10 minutes, until the pumpkin is very soft or almost mushy.

COOK'S TIP
Mutton is a mature meat with a very good flavour and texture, ideal for stews and casseroles. If mutton is not available, lamb makes a good substitute. Any dried white beans can be used instead of black-eyed beans. If a firmer texture is preferred, cook the pumpkin for about 5 minutes only, until just tender.

FISH AND PRAWNS WITH SPINACH AND COCONUT

 resh fish is combined with an unusual prawn sauce to make this a truly superb African dish.

INGREDIENTS
450g/1lb white fish fillets (cod or haddock)
15ml/1 tbsp lemon or lime juice
2.5ml/¹/₂ tsp garlic granules
5ml/1 tsp ground cinnamon
2.5ml/¹/₂ tsp dried thyme
2.5ml/¹/₂ tsp paprika
2.5ml/¹/₂ tsp freshly ground black pepper
salt
seasoned flour, for dusting
vegetable oil, for shallow frying

FOR THE SAUCE
25g/1oz/2 tbsp butter or margarine
1 onion, finely chopped
1 garlic clove, crushed
300ml/¹/₂ pint/1¹/₄ cups coconut milk
115g/4oz fresh spinach, finely sliced
225–275g/8–10oz cooked, peeled prawns
1 red chilli, seeded and finely chopped

SERVES 4

1 Place the fish in a shallow bowl and sprinkle with the lemon or lime juice.

2 Blend together the garlic granules, ground cinnamon, dried thyme, paprika, pepper and salt, and sprinkle it over the fish. Cover loosely with clear film and leave to marinate in a cool place or put in the fridge for a few hours.

3 Meanwhile, make the sauce. Melt the butter or margarine in a large saucepan and fry the onion and garlic for 5–6 minutes, until the onion is soft, stirring frequently.

4 Place the coconut milk and spinach in a separate saucepan and bring to the boil. Cook gently for a few minutes until the spinach has wilted and the coconut milk has reduced a little, then set the mixture aside to cool slightly.

5 Blend the spinach mixture in a blender or food processor for 30 seconds and add to the onion with the prawns and chopped red chilli. Stir well and simmer gently for a few minutes, then set aside while cooking the fish fillets.

6 Using a sharp knife, cut the marinated fish into 5cm/2in pieces and dip in the seasoned flour. Heat a little oil in a large frying pan and fry the fish pieces, in batches if necessary, for 2–3 minutes each side until golden brown. Drain on kitchen paper.

7 Arrange the fish on a warmed serving plate. Gently reheat the sauce and serve separately in a sauce boat or poured over the fish.

TILAPIA IN TURMERIC, MANGO AND TOMATO SAUCE

Tilapia can be found in most fishmongers. Serve this dish with yam or boiled yellow plantains.

INGREDIENTS

4 tilapia
½ lemon
2 garlic cloves, crushed
2.5ml/½ tsp dried thyme
30ml/2 tbsp chopped spring onions
vegetable oil, for shallow frying
flour, for dusting
30ml/2 tbsp groundnut oil
15g/½oz/1 tbsp butter or margarine
1 onion, finely chopped
3 tomatoes, peeled and finely chopped
5ml/1 tsp ground turmeric
60ml/4 tbsp white wine
1 green chilli, seeded and finely chopped
600ml/1 pint/2½ cups fish stock
5ml/1 tsp sugar
1 under-ripe mango, peeled and diced
salt and freshly ground black pepper
15ml/1 tbsp chopped fresh parsley,
to garnish

SERVES 4

1 Place the fish in a shallow bowl, squeeze the lemon juice over and gently rub in the garlic, thyme and some salt and pepper.

2 Place some of the spring onion in the cavity of each fish, cover with clear film and leave to marinate for a few hours.

3 Heat some oil in a frying pan, coat the fish with flour, then fry on both sides for a few minutes until golden brown. Remove with a slotted spoon and set aside.

4 Heat the groundnut oil and butter or margarine in a saucepan and fry the onion for 4–5 minutes, until soft. Stir in the tomatoes and cook briskly for a few minutes.

5 Add the turmeric, wine, chilli, fish stock and sugar, stir well and bring to the boil, then simmer gently, covered, for 10 minutes.

6 Add the fish and cook over a gentle heat for 15–20 minutes, until the fish is cooked. Arrange the mango around the fish and cook for 1–2 minutes to heat through.

7 Arrange the fish on a warmed serving plate with the mango and tomato sauce poured over. Garnish with chopped parsley and serve immediately.

TANZANIAN FISH CURRY

This delicious fish curry from Tanzania in East Africa is a national favourite and the abundance of fish available means that it is often on the menu.

INGREDIENTS
1 large snapper or red bream
1 lemon
45ml/3 tbsp vegetable oil
1 onion, finely chopped
2 garlic cloves, crushed
45ml/3 tbsp curry powder
400g/14oz can chopped tomatoes
20ml/1 heaped tbsp smooth peanut butter,
preferably unsalted
1/2 green pepper, chopped
2 slices fresh root ginger
1 green chilli, seeded and finely chopped
about 600ml/1 pint/2 1/2 cups fish stock
15ml/1 tbsp finely chopped
fresh coriander
salt and freshly ground black pepper

SERVES 2–3

1 Season the fish inside and out with salt and pepper and place in a shallow bowl. Halve the lemon and squeeze the juice all over the fish. Cover loosely with clear film and leave to marinate for at least 2 hours.

2 Heat the oil in a large non-stick saucepan and fry the onion and garlic for 5–6 minutes until soft. Reduce the heat, add the curry powder and cook, stirring, for a further 5 minutes.

3 Stir in the tomatoes and the peanut butter, mixing well, then add the green pepper, ginger, chilli and stock. Stir well and simmer gently for 10 minutes.

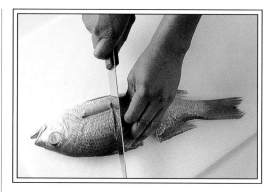

4 Cut the fish into pieces and gently lower into the sauce. Simmer for 20 minutes, or until the fish is cooked through, then using a slotted spoon, transfer the fish pieces to a plate.

5 Stir the coriander into the sauce and adjust the seasoning. If the sauce is very thick, add a little extra stock or water. Return the fish to the sauce, cook gently to heat through and serve immediately.

COOK'S TIP
The fish can be fried before adding to the sauce, if preferred. Dip in seasoned flour and fry in oil in a pan or a wok for a few minutes before adding to the sauce.

BAKED RED SNAPPER

Y ou can vary the amount of sauce to serve with this dish each time you make it – for less sauce, just remove the foil after cooking for 20 minutes and continue baking, uncovered.

INGREDIENTS
1 large red snapper, cleaned
juice of 1 lemon
2.5ml/¹/₂ tsp paprika
2.5ml/¹/₂ tsp garlic granules
2.5ml/¹/₂ tsp dried thyme
2.5ml/¹/₂ tsp freshly ground black pepper
cooked rice and lemon wedges, to serve

FOR THE SAUCE
30ml/2 tbsp palm or vegetable oil
1 onion
400g/14oz can chopped tomatoes
2 garlic cloves
1 thyme sprig or 2.5ml/¹/₂ tsp
dried thyme
1 green chilli, seeded and finely chopped
¹/₂ green pepper, seeded and chopped
300ml/¹/₂ pint/1¹/₄ cups fish stock
or water

SERVES 3–4

1 Preheat the oven to 200°C/400°F/Gas 6. For the sauce, heat the oil in a saucepan, fry the onion for 5 minutes, then add the tomatoes, garlic, thyme and chilli.

2 Add the green pepper and fish stock or water. Bring to the boil, stirring, then reduce the heat and simmer, covered, for about 10 minutes, or until the vegetables are soft. Leave to cool a little, then place in a blender or food processor and blend to a smooth purée.

3 Wash the fish well, then score the skin with a sharp knife in a criss-cross pattern. Mix together the lemon juice, paprika, garlic, thyme and black pepper, spoon over the fish and rub in well.

4 Place the fish in a greased baking dish and pour the sauce over the top. Cover with foil and bake for about 30–40 minutes, or until the fish is cooked and flakes easily when tested with a knife. Serve with boiled rice and lemon wedges.

FRIED POMFRET IN COCONUT SAUCE

nce again, the distinct flavour of coconut is used to make this an African dish to remember.

INGREDIENTS
4 pomfret
1 lemon
5ml/1 tsp garlic granules
vegetable oil, for shallow frying
salt and freshly ground black pepper

FOR THE COCONUT SAUCE
450ml/³/₄ pint/1⁷/₈ cups water
2 thin slices fresh root ginger
25–40g/1–1¹/₂ oz creamed coconut
30ml/2 tbsp vegetable oil
1 red onion, sliced
2 garlic cloves, crushed
1 green chilli, seeded and thinly sliced
15ml/1 tbsp chopped fresh coriander

SERVES 4

1 Cut the fish in half and sprinkle inside and out with the juice from the lemon. Season with the garlic granules and salt and pepper. Leave to marinate for a few hours.

2 Heat a little oil in a large frying pan. Pat away the excess lemon juice from the fish, then fry in the oil for 10 minutes, turning once. Set aside.

3 To make the sauce, place the water in a saucepan with the slices of ginger, bring to the boil and simmer until the liquid is reduced to just over 300ml/½ pint/1¼ cups. Take out the ginger and reserve, then add the creamed coconut to the pan and stir until the coconut has melted.

4 Heat the oil in a wok or large pan and fry the onion and garlic for 2–3 minutes. Add the reserved ginger and coconut stock, the chilli and coriander, stir well and then gently add the fish. Simmer for 10 minutes, until the fish is cooked through.

5 Transfer the fish to a warmed serving plate, adjust the seasoning for the sauce and pour over the fish. Serve immediately.

DONU'S LOBSTER PIRI PIRI

 obster in its shell, in true Nigerian style, flavoured with a dried shrimp piri piri sauce.

INGREDIENTS

60ml/4 tbsp vegetable oil
2 onions, chopped
5ml/1 tsp chopped fresh root ginger
450g/1lb fresh or canned
tomatoes, chopped
15ml/1 tbsp tomato purée
225g/8oz cooked, peeled prawns
10ml/2 tsp ground coriander
1 green chilli, seeded and chopped
15ml/1 tbsp ground dried shrimps
or crayfish
600ml/1 pint/2½ cups water
1 green pepper, seeded and sliced
2 cooked lobsters, halved
salt and freshly ground black pepper
fresh coriander sprigs, to garnish
cooked rice, to serve

SERVES 2–4

1 Heat the oil in a large non-stick saucepan and fry the onions, ginger, tomatoes and tomato purée for 5 minutes, or until the onions are soft.

2 Add the prawns, ground coriander, chilli and ground shrimps or crayfish and stir well to mix.

3 Stir in the water, green pepper and salt and pepper, bring to the boil and simmer, uncovered, over a moderate heat for about 20–30 minutes until the sauce is reduced.

4 Add the lobsters to the sauce and cook for a few minutes to heat through. Arrange each lobster half on a bed of fluffy white rice and pour over the sauce. Garnish with coriander and serve immediately.

EGUSI SPINACH AND EGG

This is a superbly balanced dish for non-meat eaters. Egusi, or ground melon seed, is widely used in West African cooking, adding a creamy texture and a nutty flavour to many recipes. It is especially good with fresh spinach.

INGREDIENTS
900g/2lb fresh spinach
115g/4oz ground egusi
90ml/6 tbsp groundnut or vegetable oil
4 tomatoes, peeled and chopped
1 onion, chopped
2 garlic cloves, crushed
1 slice fresh root ginger, finely chopped
150ml/¼ pint/⅔ cup vegetable stock
1 red chilli, seeded and finely chopped
salt
6 eggs

SERVES 4

COOK'S TIP
Instead of using boiled eggs, you could make an omelette flavoured with herbs and garlic. Serve it either whole or sliced, with the egusi sauce. If you can't find egusi, use ground almonds as a substitute.

1 Roll the spinach into bundles and cut into strips. Place in a bowl.

2 Cover the spinach with boiling water, then drain through a sieve. Press with your fingers to remove excess water.

3 Place the egusi in a bowl and gradually add enough water to form a paste, stirring all the time.

4 Heat the oil in a saucepan, add the tomatoes, onion, garlic and ginger and fry over a moderate heat for 10 minutes, stirring frequently.

5 Add the egusi paste, stock, chilli and salt, cook for 10 minutes, then add the spinach and stir into the sauce. Cook for 15 minutes, uncovered, stirring frequently.

6 Meanwhile, hard-boil the eggs, stand in cold water for a few minutes to cool, then shell and cut in half. Arrange in a shallow serving dish and pour the egusi spinach over the top. Serve hot.

MAKANDE

 traditional dish from Uparie-Tanzania that can be served with meat, fish or simply a salad.

INGREDIENTS
225g/8oz/1¼ cups red kidney beans,
soaked overnight
1 onion, chopped
2 garlic cloves, crushed
75g/3oz creamed coconut
225g/8oz/1⅓ cups frozen sweetcorn
300ml/½ pint/1¼ cups vegetable stock
or water
salt and freshly ground black pepper

SERVES 3–4

1 Drain the kidney beans and place in a pan. Cover the beans with water and boil rapidly for 15 minutes. Reduce the heat and continue boiling for about 1 hour, until the beans are tender, adding more water if necessary. Drain and discard the cooking liquid.

2 Place the beans in a clean pan with the onion, garlic, coconut, sweetcorn and salt and pepper.

3 Add the stock or water, bring to the boil and simmer for 20 minutes, stirring occasionally to dissolve the coconut.

4 Adjust the seasoning and spoon into a warmed serving dish.

VEGETABLES IN PEANUT SAUCE

Palm oil, a much-used African ingredient, gives this dish a distinct flavour; if you prefer, however, you can use an oil with less flavour instead.

INGREDIENTS

15ml/1 tbsp palm or vegetable oil
1 onion, chopped
2 garlic cloves, crushed
400g/14oz can tomatoes, puréed
45ml/3 tbsp smooth peanut butter,
preferably unsalted
750ml/1¼ pints/3⅔ cups water
5ml/1 tsp dried thyme
1 green chilli, seeded and chopped
1 vegetable stock cube
2.5ml/½ tsp ground allspice
salt
2 carrots
115g/4oz white cabbage
175g/6oz okra
½ red pepper
150ml/¼ pint/⅔ cup vegetable stock

SERVES 4

1 Heat the oil in a large non-stick saucepan and fry the onion and garlic over a moderate heat for 5 minutes, stirring frequently. Add the tomatoes and peanut butter and stir well.

2 Stir in the water, thyme, chilli, stock cube, allspice and a little salt. Bring to the boil then simmer gently, uncovered, for about 35 minutes.

3 Meanwhile, cut the carrots into sticks, slice the cabbage, top and tail the okra and seed and slice the red pepper.

4 Place the vegetables in a saucepan with the stock, bring to the boil and cook until tender but still with a little "bite".

5 Drain the vegetables and place them in a warmed serving dish. Pour the peanut sauce over the top and serve.

CHICK-PEAS, SWEET POTATO AND GARDEN EGG

G arden egg is a small variety of aubergine used widely in West Africa. It is round and white, which may explain its other name – eggplant.

INGREDIENTS
45ml/3 tbsp olive oil
1 red onion, chopped
3 garlic cloves, crushed
115g/4oz sweet potatoes, peeled and diced
3 garden eggs or 1 large aubergine, diced
425g/15oz can chick-peas, drained
5ml/1 tsp dried tarragon
2.5ml/¹/₂ tsp dried thyme
5ml/1 tsp ground cumin
5ml/1 tsp ground turmeric
2.5ml/¹/₂ tsp ground allspice
*5 canned plum tomatoes, chopped with
60ml/4 tbsp reserved juice*
6 dried apricots
*600ml/1 pint/2¹/₂ cups well-flavoured
vegetable stock*
1 green chilli, seeded and finely chopped
30ml/2 tbsp chopped fresh coriander
salt and freshly ground black pepper

SERVES 3–4

1 Heat the olive oil in a large pan over a moderate heat. Add the onion, garlic and sweet potatoes and cook for about 5 minutes until the onion is slightly softened.

2 Stir in the garden eggs or aubergine, then add the chick-peas and the herbs and spices. Stir well to mix and cook over a gentle heat for a few minutes.

3 Add the tomatoes and their juice, the apricots, stock, chilli and seasoning. Stir well, bring slowly to the boil and cook for about 15 minutes.

4 When the sweet potatoes are tender, add the coriander, stir and adjust the seasoning, if necessary, and serve.

BEAN AND GARI LOAF

his recipe is a newly created vegetarian dish using typical Ghanaian flavours and ingredients.

INGREDIENTS
225g/8oz/1¹/₄ cups red kidney beans, soaked overnight
15g/¹/₂oz/1 tbsp butter or margarine
1 onion, finely chopped
2 garlic cloves, crushed
¹/₂ red pepper, seeded and chopped
¹/₂ green pepper, seeded and chopped
1 green chilli, seeded and finely chopped
5ml/1 tsp mixed chopped herbs
2 eggs
15ml/1 tbsp lemon juice
75ml/5 tbsp gari
salt and freshly ground black pepper

SERVES 4

COOK'S TIP
Gari is a course-grained flour used as a staple food in a similar way to ground rice. Gari is made from a starchy root vegetable, cassava, which is first dried, then ground.

1 Drain the beans, place in a pan, cover with water and boil for 15 minutes. Reduce the heat and boil for 1 hour, or until the beans are tender. Drain, reserving the cooking liquid. Grease a 900g/2lb loaf tin and preheat the oven to 190°C/375°F/Gas 5.

2 Melt the butter or margarine and fry the onion, garlic and peppers for 5 minutes. Add the chilli, herbs and seasoning.

3 Place the cooked kidney beans in a bowl and mash to a pulp. Add the onion and pepper mixture and stir well. Cool slightly, then stir in the eggs and lemon juice.

4 Place the gari in a separate bowl and sprinkle generously with warm water. The gari should become soft and fluffy after about 5 minutes.

5 Pour the gari into the bean and onion mixture and stir together thoroughly. If the consistency is too stiff, add a little of the bean liquid. Spoon the mixture into the prepared loaf tin and bake in the oven for 35–45 minutes, until firm to the touch.

6 Cool the loaf in the tin before turning it out on to a plate. Cut into thick slices and serve.

BLACK-EYED BEAN STEW WITH SPICY PUMPKIN

This colourful African stew has a wonderfully spicy flavour that cheers up a cold winter's day.

INGREDIENTS

*225g/8oz/1¼ cups black-eyed beans,
soaked overnight and drained
1 onion, chopped
1 pepper, seeded and chopped
2 garlic cloves, crushed
1 vegetable stock cube
1 fresh thyme sprig
5ml/1 tsp paprika
2.5ml/½ tsp mixed spice
2 carrots, sliced
15–30ml/1–2 tbsp palm oil
700g/1½lb pumpkin
1 onion
15g/½oz/2 tbsp butter or margarine
2 garlic cloves, crushed
3 tomatoes, peeled and chopped
2.5ml/½ tsp ground cinnamon
10ml/2 tsp curry powder
pinch of grated nutmeg
300ml/½ pint/⅔ cup water
salt, hot pepper sauce and freshly ground
black pepper*

SERVES 3–4

1 Bring the beans to the boil, then add the onion, pepper, garlic, stock cube, thyme, paprika and mixed spice. Simmer for about 45 minutes, or until the beans are tender. Add salt and a little hot pepper sauce.

2 Add the carrots and palm oil and continue cooking for 10–12 minutes until the carrots are cooked, adding a little more water if necessary. Remove from the heat and set aside.

3 To make the spicy pumpkin, cut the pumpkin into cubes and finely chop the onion.

4 Melt the butter or margarine in a frying pan or saucepan, then add the pumpkin, onion, garlic, tomatoes, spices and water. Stir well to combine and simmer until the pumpkin is soft. Season with salt, hot pepper sauce and black pepper, to taste. Serve with the cooked black-eyed beans.

BULGUR AND PINE NUT PILAFF

Pilaff is a popular staple in the Middle East, and here is a North African version. Serve it with a vegetable or meat stew to make a truly satisfying meal.

INGREDIENTS

30ml/2 tbsp olive oil
1 onion, chopped
1 garlic clove, crushed
5ml/1 tsp ground saffron or turmeric
2.5ml/¹/₂ tsp ground cinnamon
1 green chilli, seeded and chopped
600ml/1 pint/2¹/₂ cups vegetable stock
150ml/¹/₄ pint/²/₃ cup white wine
225g/8oz/1¹/₃ cups bulgur wheat
15g/¹/₂oz/1 tbsp butter or margarine
30–45ml/2–3 tbsp pine nuts
30ml/2 tbsp chopped fresh parsley

SERVES 4

1 Heat the olive oil in a large saucepan and fry the onion until soft. Add the garlic, ground saffron or turmeric, cinnamon and chilli and fry for a few seconds more.

2 Add the stock and wine, bring to the boil, then simmer for 8 minutes.

3 Rinse the bulgur wheat under cold water, drain and add to the stock. Cover and simmer gently for about 15 minutes until the stock is absorbed.

4 Melt the butter or margarine in a small pan, add the pine nuts and fry for a few minutes until golden. Add to the bulgur wheat with the chopped parsley and stir with a fork to mix.

5 Spoon into a warmed serving dish and serve hot.

COOK'S TIP
You can leave out the wine, if you prefer, and replace it with water or stock. It's not essential, but it adds extra flavour.

CAMEROON COCONUT RICE

T his version of a favourite African dish, Coconut Joloff, can be left moist, like a risotto, or cooked longer for a drier result.

INGREDIENTS
30ml/2 tbsp vegetable oil
1 onion, chopped
30ml/2 tbsp tomato purée
600ml/1 pint/2¹/₂ cups coconut milk
2 carrots
1 yellow pepper
5ml/1 tsp dried thyme
2.5ml/¹/₂ tsp mixed spice
1 fresh green chilli, seeded and chopped
350g/12oz/1¹/₂ cups long grain rice
salt
coconut shreds, to garnish

SERVES 4

1 Heat the oil in a large saucepan and fry the onion for 2 minutes. Add the tomato purée and cook over a moderate heat for 5–6 minutes, stirring all the time. Add the coconut milk, stir well and bring to the boil.

2 Roughly chop the carrots and chop the pepper, discarding the seeds.

3 Stir the carrots, pepper, thyme, mixed spice, chilli and rice into the onion mixture, season with salt and bring to the boil. Cover and cook over a low heat until the rice has absorbed most of the liquid. Cover the rice with foil, secure with the lid and steam very gently until the rice is done. Serve hot, garnished with coconut shreds.

KENYAN MUNG BEAN STEW

The Kenyan name for this simple and tasty stew made from dried mung beans is *Dengu*.

INGREDIENTS
225g/8oz/1¼ cups mung beans, soaked overnight
25g/1oz/2 tbsp ghee or butter
2 garlic cloves, crushed
1 red onion, chopped
30ml/2 tbsp tomato purée
½ green pepper, seeded and cut into small cubes
½ red pepper, seeded and cut into small cubes
1 green chilli, seeded and finely chopped
300ml/½ pint/1¼ cups water

SERVES 4

COOK'S TIP
If you prefer a more traditional, smoother texture, cook the mung beans until very soft, then mash them thoroughly until smooth.

1 Put the mung beans in a large saucepan, cover with water and boil until the beans are soft and the water has evaporated. Remove from the heat and mash roughly with a fork or potato masher.

2 Heat the ghee or butter in a separate saucepan, add the garlic and onion and fry for 4–5 minutes until golden brown, then add the tomato purée and cook for a further 2–3 minutes, stirring all the time.

3 Stir in the mashed beans, then the green and red peppers and chilli.

4 Add the water, stirring well to mix all the ingredients together.

5 Pour back into a clean saucepan and simmer for about 10 minutes, then spoon into a serving dish and serve at once.

GROUND RICE

round rice is a staple dish in West Africa, where it is often served with soups and stews.

INGREDIENTS
300ml/¹/₂ pint/1¹/₄ cups water
25g/1oz/2 tbsp butter or margarine
300ml/¹/₂ pint/1¹/₄ cups milk
2.5ml/¹/₂ tsp salt
15ml/1 tbsp chopped fresh parsley
275g/10oz/1¹/₂ cups ground rice

SERVES 4

1 Place the water, butter or margarine and milk in a saucepan, bring to the boil and add the salt and parsley.

2 Add the ground rice, stirring vigorously with a wooden spoon to prevent the rice becoming lumpy.

3 Cover the pan and cook over a low heat for about 15 minutes, beating the mixture regularly every two minutes to prevent lumps forming.

4 To test if the rice is cooked, rub a pinch of the mixture between your fingers; if it feels smooth and fairly dry, it is ready. Serve the rice dish hot.

COOK'S TIP
Ground rice is creamy white and when cooked has a slightly grainy texture. Although often used here in sweet dishes, it is a tasty grain to serve with savoury dishes too. The addition of milk makes it creamier, but it can be omitted if preferred.

MANDAZI

erve these East African breads either as a snack or as an accompaniment to a meal.

INGREDIENTS

4 or 5 cardamom pods
450g/1lb/4 cups self-raising flour
45ml/3 tbsp caster sugar
5ml/1 tsp baking powder
1 egg, beaten
30ml/2 tbsp vegetable oil, plus extra for deep frying
225ml/7fl oz/⅞ cup milk or water

MAKES ABOUT 15

2 Put the egg and oil in a small bowl and beat together, then add to the flour mixture. Mix with your fingers, gradually adding the milk or water to make a dough.

3 Lightly knead the dough until smooth and not sticky when a finger is pushed into it, adding more flour if necessary. Leave in a warm place for 15 minutes.

4 Roll out the dough to about a 1cm/½in thickness and cut into 6cm/2½in rounds. Heat the oil and deep fry the mandazis for 4–5 minutes, until golden brown, turning frequently in the oil.

1 Crush each cardamom pod, shake out the seeds and grind them in a small pestle and mortar. Place in a large bowl with the flour, sugar and baking powder. Stir well.

PLANTAIN AND GREEN BANANA SALAD

The plantains and bananas may be cooked in their skins to retain their soft texture. They will then absorb all the flavour of the dressing.

INGREDIENTS

2 firm yellow plantains
3 green bananas
1 garlic clove, crushed
1 red onion
15–30ml/1–2 tbsp chopped
fresh coriander
45ml/3 tbsp sunflower oil
22.5ml/1½ tbsp malt vinegar
salt and freshly ground black pepper

SERVES 4

1 Slit the plantains and bananas lengthwise along their natural ridges, then cut in half and place in a large saucepan.

2 Cover the plantains and bananas with water, add a little salt and bring to the boil. Boil gently for 20 minutes until tender, then remove from the water. When they are cool enough to handle, peel and cut into medium-size slices.

3 Put the plantain and banana slices into a bowl and add the garlic, turning to mix.

4 Halve the onion and slice thinly. Add to the bowl with the coriander, oil, vinegar and seasoning. Toss together to mix and then serve.

ETHIOPIAN COLLARD GREENS

Also known as *Abesha Gomen*, this dish is simple and delicious. Use spring greens in place of the collard greens if you are unable to get the real thing.

INGREDIENTS
450g/1lb collard greens
60ml/4 tbsp olive oil
2 small red onions, finely chopped
1 garlic clove, crushed
2.5ml/¹⁄₂ tsp grated fresh root ginger
2 green chillies, seeded and sliced
150ml/¹⁄₄ pint/²⁄₃ cup vegetable stock
or water
1 red pepper, seeded and sliced
salt and freshly ground black pepper

SERVES 4

COOK'S TIP
Traditionally, this dish is cooked with more liquid and for longer. Here, the cooking time has been reduced from 45 to 15 minutes. However, if you fancy a more authentic taste, cook for longer and increase the amount of liquid. Green cabbage is a good substitute for collard greens.

1 Wash the collard greens, then strip the leaves from the stalks and steam the leaves over a pan of boiling water for about 5 minutes until slightly wilted. Set aside on a plate to cool, then place in a sieve or colander and press out the excess water.

2 Using a large sharp knife, slice the collard greens very thinly.

3 Heat the oil in a saucepan and fry the onions until browned. Add the garlic and ginger and stir-fry with the onions for a few minutes, then add the chillies and a little of the stock or water and cook for 2 minutes.

4 Add the greens, red pepper and the remaining stock or water. Season with salt and pepper, mix well, then cover and cook over a low heat for about 15 minutes.

GREEN LENTIL SALAD

A *zifa* is the African name for this piquant, colourful salad. It is best served as an accompaniment to a meat or fish dish.

INGREDIENTS
225g/8oz/1 cup green lentils,
soaked overnight
2 tomatoes, peeled and chopped
1 red onion, finely chopped
1 green chilli, seeded and chopped
60ml/4 tbsp lemon juice
75ml/5 tbsp olive oil
2.5ml/¹/₂ tsp prepared mustard
salt and freshly ground black pepper
lettuce leaves, to garnish

SERVES 4

1 Drain the lentils and place them in a saucepan, cover with water and bring to the boil. Simmer for 45 minutes until soft, drain, then tip into a bowl and mash lightly with a potato masher.

2 Add the chopped tomatoes, onion, chilli, lemon juice, olive oil, mustard and seasoning. Mix well, adjust the seasoning if necessary, then chill before serving the salad garnished with lettuce leaves.

PAWPAW AND MANGO WITH MANGO CREAM

Mangoes vary tremendously in size. If you can only find small ones, buy three instead of two for this refreshing dessert.

INGREDIENTS
2 large ripe mangoes
300ml/¹/₂ pint/1¹/₂ cups extra thick double cream
8 dried apricots, halved
150ml/¹/₄ pint/²/₃ cup orange juice or water
1 ripe pawpaw

SERVES 4

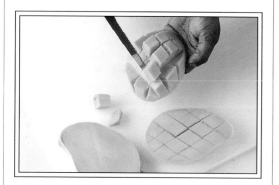

1 Take one thick slice from one of the mangoes and, while still on the skin, slash the flesh with a sharp knife in a criss-cross pattern to make cubes.

2 Turn the piece of mango inside-out and cut away the cubed flesh from the skin. Place in a bowl, mash with a fork to a pulp, then add the cream and mix together well. Spoon into a freezer tub and freeze for about 1–1¹/₂ hours until half frozen.

3 Meanwhile, put the apricots and orange juice or water in a small saucepan. Bring to the boil, then simmer gently until the apricots are soft, adding a little more juice or water if necessary, so that the apricots remain moist. Remove from the heat and set aside to cool.

4 Chop or dice the remaining mango as above and place in a bowl. Cut the pawpaw in half, remove the seeds and peel. Dice the flesh and add to the mango.

5 Pour the apricot sauce over the fruit and gently toss to coat all the fruit.

6 Stir the semi-frozen mango cream a few times until spoonable but not soft. Serve the fruit topped with the mango cream.

BANANA AND MELON IN ORANGE VANILLA SAUCE

Most large supermarkets and health food shops sell vanilla pods. If vanilla pods are hard to find, use a few drops of natural vanilla essence instead.

INGREDIENTS

300ml/¹/₂ pint/1¹/₄ cups orange juice
1 vanilla pod or a few drops of
vanilla essence
5ml/1 tsp grated orange rind
15ml/1 tbsp sugar
4 bananas
1 honeydew melon
30ml/2 tbsp lemon juice
orange rind shreds, to decorate

SERVES 4

1 Place the orange juice in a small saucepan with the vanilla pod, orange rind and sugar and gently bring to the boil.

2 Reduce the heat and simmer gently for 15 minutes or until the sauce is syrupy. Remove from the heat and leave to cool. If using vanilla essence, stir into the sauce once it has cooled.

3 Roughly chop the bananas and melon, place in a large serving bowl and toss with the lemon juice.

4 Pour the cooled sauce over the fruit and chill before serving, decorated with shreds of fresh orange rind.

BANANA MANDAZI

his is one of the most popular of African desserts – simple to make and delicious to eat!

INGREDIENTS
1 egg
2 ripe bananas, roughly chopped
150ml/¼ pint/⅔ cup milk
2.5ml/½ tsp vanilla essence
225g/8oz/2 cups self-raising flour
5ml/1 tsp baking powder
45ml/3 tbsp sugar
vegetable oil, for deep frying
icing sugar, to decorate

SERVES 4

1 Place the egg, bananas, milk, vanilla essence, flour, baking powder and sugar in a blender or food processor.

2 Process to make a smooth batter. It should have a creamy dropping consistency. If it is too thick, add a little extra milk. Set aside for 10 minutes.

3 Heat the oil in a heavy saucepan or deep-fat fryer. When hot, carefully place spoonfuls of the mixture in the oil and fry, in batches, for 3–4 minutes until golden.

4 Remove with a slotted spoon and drain on kitchen paper. Keep warm, then serve them all at once, sprinkled with icing sugar.

TROPICAL FRUIT PANCAKES

ring a touch of tropical sunshine into your kitchen with these fruit-filled pancakes.

INGREDIENTS
115g/4oz/1 cup self-raising flour
pinch of grated nutmeg
15ml/1 tbsp caster sugar
1 egg
300ml/½ pint/1¼ cups milk
15ml/1 tbsp melted butter or margarine,
plus extra for frying
15ml/1 tbsp fine desiccated
coconut (optional)
icing sugar, to decorate
fresh cream, to serve

FOR THE FILLING
225g/8oz ripe, firm mango
2 bananas
2 kiwi fruit
1 large orange
15ml/1 tbsp lemon juice
30ml/2 tbsp orange juice
15ml/1 tbsp honey
30–45ml/2–3 tbsp orange
liqueur (optional)

SERVES 4

1 Sift the flour, nutmeg and caster sugar into a large mixing bowl. In a separate bowl, beat the egg lightly, then beat in most of the milk. Add to the flour mixture and beat with a wooden spoon to make a thick, smooth batter.

2 Add the remaining milk, butter or margarine and coconut, if using, and continue beating until the batter is smooth and of a fairly thin, dropping consistency.

3 Melt a little butter or margarine in a large non-stick frying pan. Swirl to cover the pan, then pour in some batter to cover the base of the pan. Fry the pancake until golden brown, then toss or turn with a spatula. Repeat with the remaining mixture to make about eight pancakes.

4 Dice the mango, roughly chop the bananas and slice the kiwi fruit. Cut away the peel and pith from the orange and cut into segments.

5 Place the fruit in a bowl. Mix the lemon and orange juices, honey and liqueur, if using, then pour over the fruit.

6 Spoon some fruit along the centre of a pancake and fold over each side. Repeat with the others, then arrange on a plate, dredge with sugar and serve with cream.

INDEX